MW01688273

ANSWER ME THIS, WORLD BOOK

If you sneeze with your eyes open, will they pop out?

World Book answers YOUR questions - about - fear and danger

WORLD BOOK

www.worldbook.com

How dangerous are llamas?

Do you know the phrase "Save the drama for your llama"?

Well, you shouldn't follow this rule. Don't save your drama for anyone—and that includes your llama. When a llama is angry or under attack, it spits bad-smelling saliva in its enemy's face. But llamas are pretty even-tempered most of the time. Which can't be said of drama queens.

Friend or foe?

Why do we have nightmares?

To make sleep more exciting.

Actually, a number of factors can cause nightmares. They tend to occur in times of stress. They may also follow a hurtful or shocking experience. You might have nightmares after watching horror films or television shows. And you might have night**mares** when riding a horse after dark.

What is a phobia?

A phobia is a fear of something specific.

For example, decidophobia is the fear of making decisions.

Can animals smell fear?

Animals can sense fear more than smell it.

Let's use dogs as an example. Dogs are known for two things: being super-good cuddlers and being super-good smellers. One thing they are especially good at smelling is sweat. Humans release a certain type of sweat when they are nervous or afraid. Dogs also use other cues to determine whether someone is fearful. For instance, a person's movements and body language can indicate that they are afraid. So dogs can use smell and actions to know that someone is fearful and *does not* want to cuddle.

How will the world end, according to science?

Scientists have a few ideas.

Earth's core might cool. Or the sun could die and expand. Or the universe could burst into pieces. Any of these would be a long way off. No need to worry about the sky falling today, Chicken Little.

Will dropping **a penny** from the top of the Empire State Building kill somebody on the ground?

2

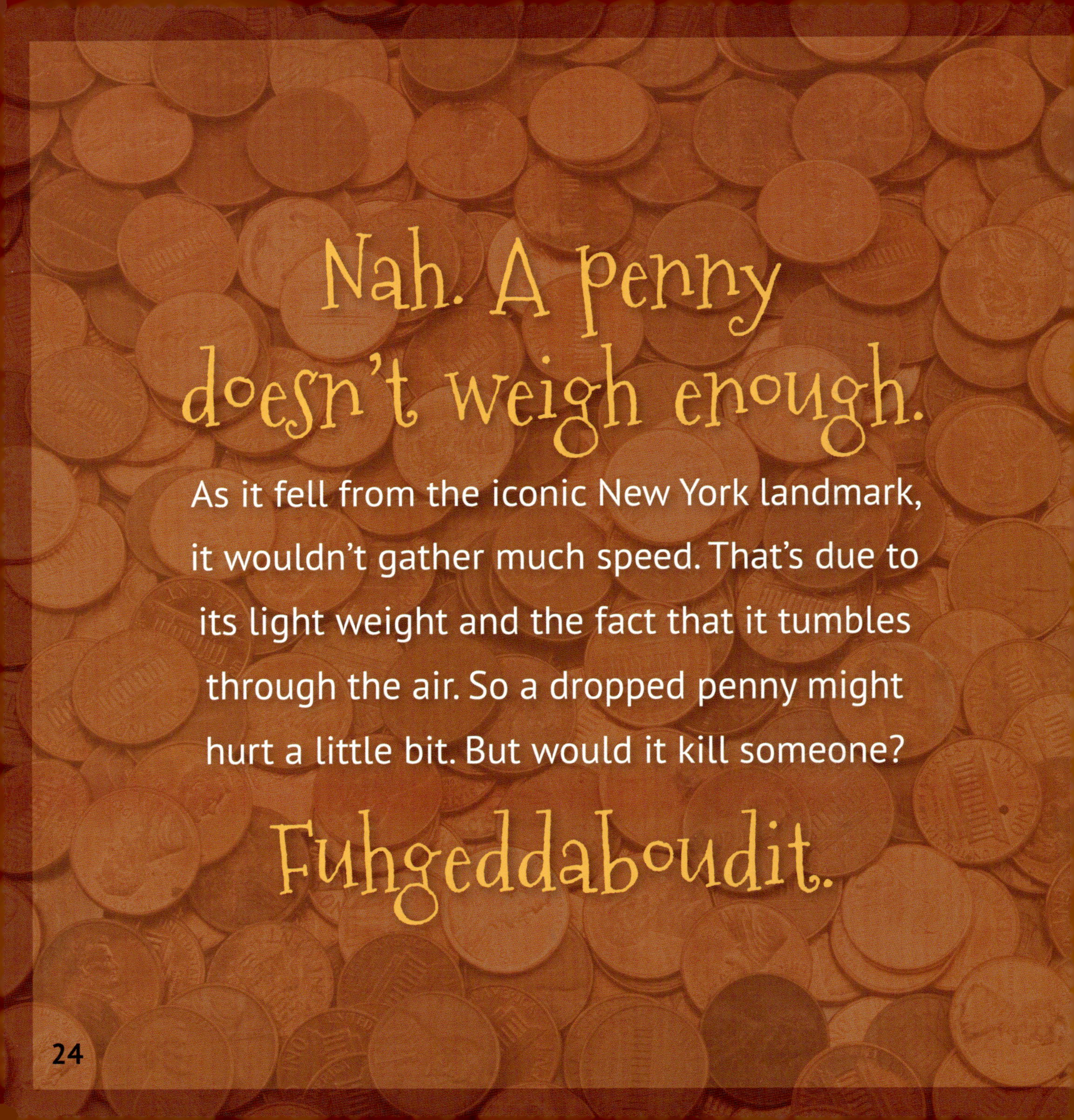

Nah. A penny doesn't weigh enough.

As it fell from the iconic New York landmark, it wouldn't gather much speed. That's due to its light weight and the fact that it tumbles through the air. So a dropped penny might hurt a little bit. But would it kill someone?

Fuhgeddaboudit.

What eye color is the most **dangerous** to have?

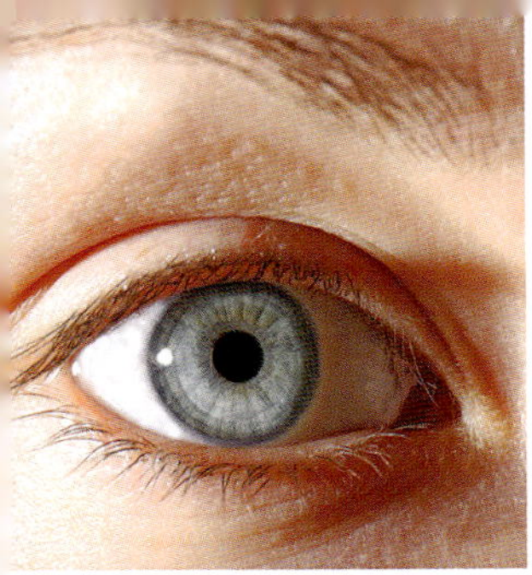
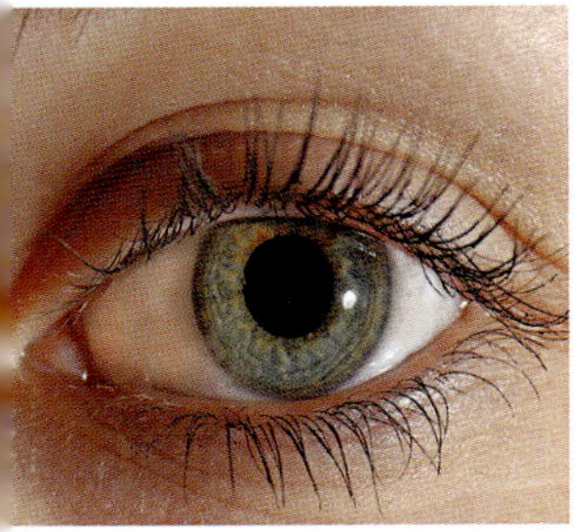
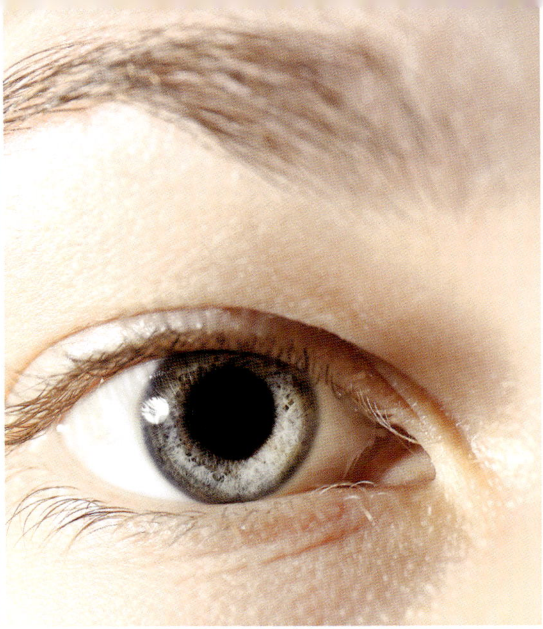
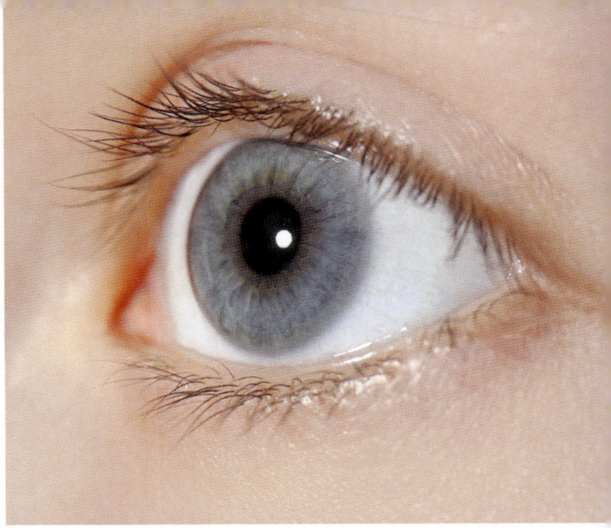

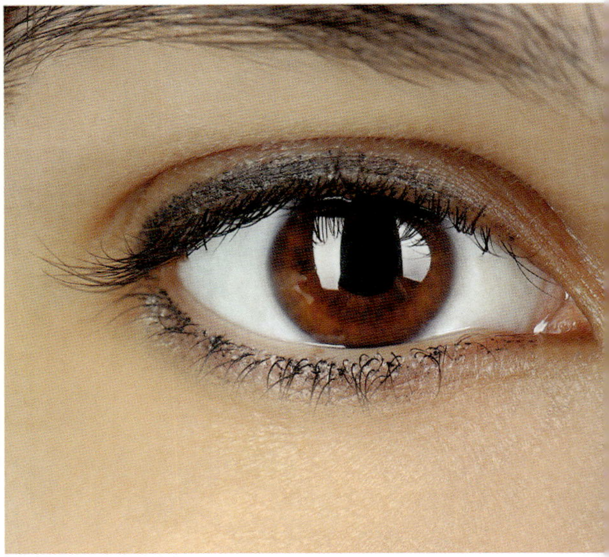
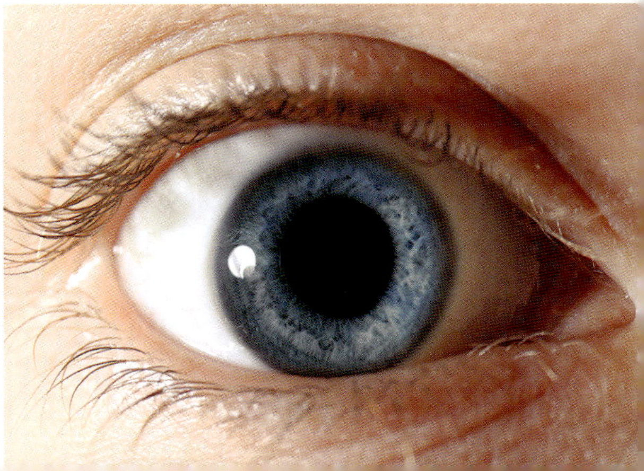

No eye color is dangerous—for you or anyone else.

Did you just reach for your eyes? People with light-colored eyes have less melanin than people with dark-colored eyes. Melanin is a brownish-black substance that absorbs strong light. So people with light eyes—say, blue eyes—might be more sensitive to light than those with brown eyes.

Does your heart stop when you sneeze?

No way.

Not even when an old man sneezes so loud, it scares everyone on the bus! Your heartbeat may adjust slightly to accommodate the sneeze. But a healthy heart never stops beating.

I'm OK, buddy!

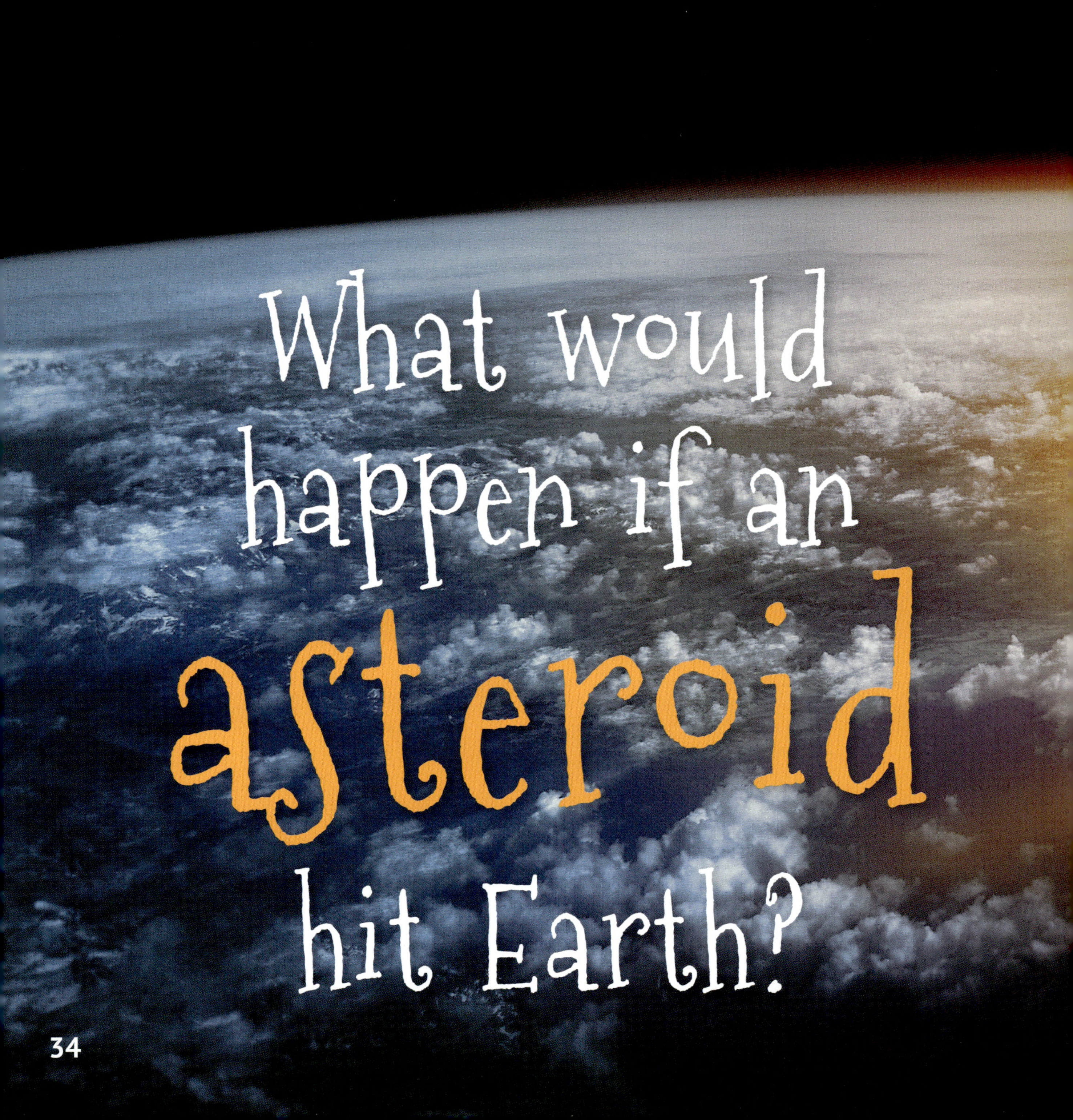

What would happen if an asteroid hit Earth?

Nothing good.

Asteroids are rocky objects that orbit our sun. A large asteroid striking Earth would cause a huge explosion and kick large amounts of dust into the atmosphere. The dust could block sunlight and darken the skies for many months. Many plants and animals would become extinct. Luckily, large strikes are very rare.

How do dolphins sleep without drowning?

Very carefully.

When dolphins sleep, one half of the brain sleeps and one half stays awake and controls breathing. Each side gets about four hours of sleep, and then the dolphin switches sides. Don't try this method on **porpoise**—this is not how humans sleep, so your brain would **flip** out.

Zzzzz

Do alligators bite?

Alligators drag animals underwater to drown them and tear them to pieces. They tear their prey apart by grabbing hold of the animal with their jaws. They then spin the prey's body until the part they're holding twists off.

So, yes, they bite.

A A A A A A

Does cracking your knuckles cause arthritis?

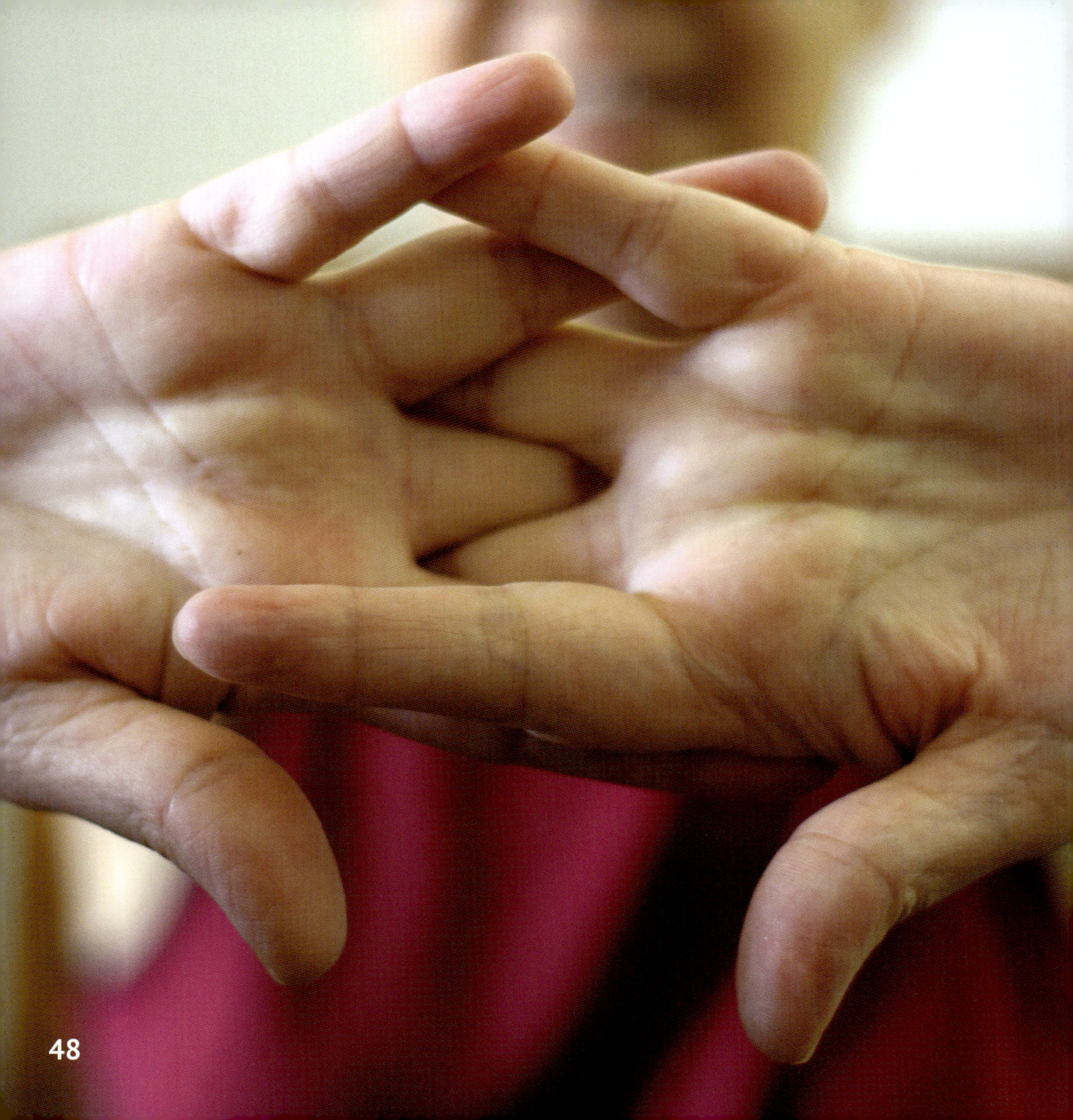

No.

Arthritis is a term for pain and stiffness of the joints, the places where bones meet. People crack their knuckles for a bunch of reasons. They might want their knuckles to feel looser. Or, they might simply want to annoy other people. (No one wants to hear your insides!) There *are* some consequences to cracking your knuckles, though. Repetitive cracking may reduce grip strength.

Do frogs contain a deadly poison?

Some do.

Tiny, colorful poison dart frogs live in the rain forests of Central and South America. Their skin produces a deadly poison that has been used in blowgun darts.

If you sneeze with your eyes open, will they

pop out?

No way. Your eye muscles are very strong.

In fact, they are so strong that you can do upwards of 100 million eye rolls at your embarrassing parents. Also, the muscles that you use when you sneeze aren't connected to your eyes. Now, if your eyes *did* pop out when you sneezed, that would be quite a **spectacle.**

WOW!

What makes spiders dangerous?

One word: poison.

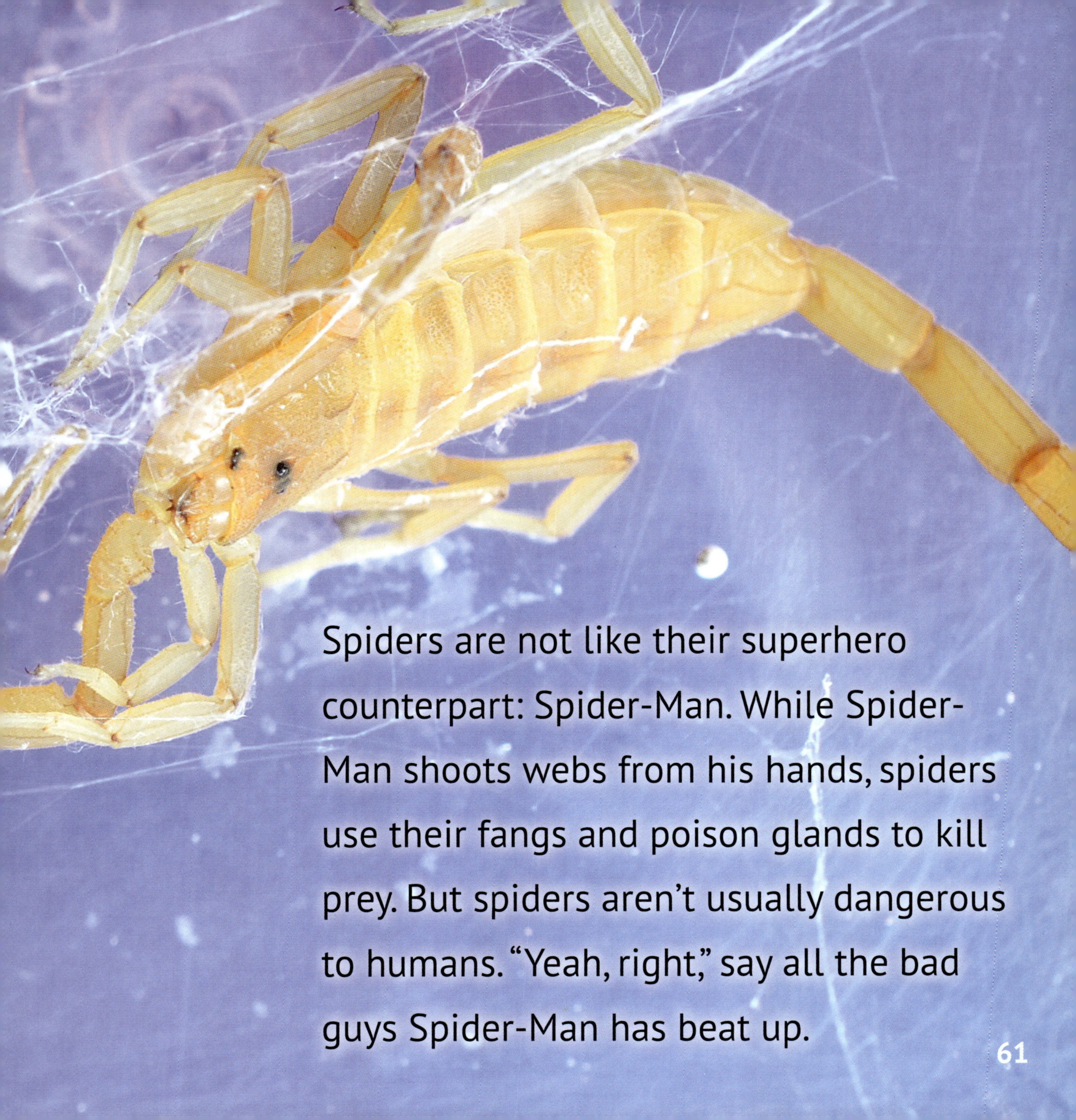

Spiders are not like their superhero counterpart: Spider-Man. While Spider-Man shoots webs from his hands, spiders use their fangs and poison glands to kill prey. But spiders aren't usually dangerous to humans. "Yeah, right," say all the bad guys Spider-Man has beat up.

Is it really dangerous to wake someone when they are sleepwalking?

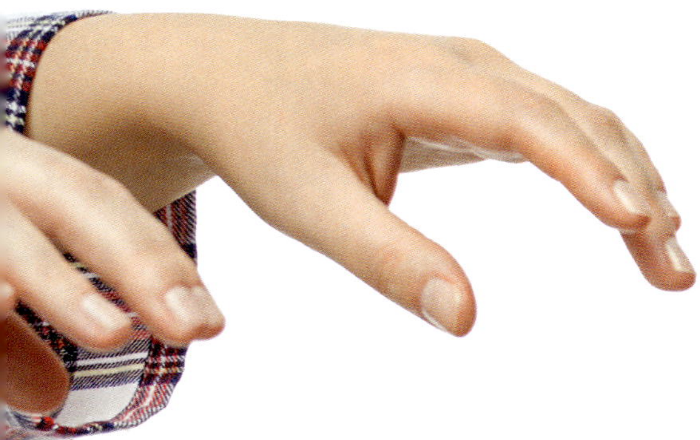

Nope.

Most sleepwalkers don't actually walk at all. They sit up in bed or stand. People who sleepwalk are also called *somnambulists*. It does not harm a sleepwalker to be awakened. So don't worry, you won't have to call *some ambulance*.

What would happen if I was sucked into a black hole?

You'd better make yourself nice and comfortable, because you're not coming out.

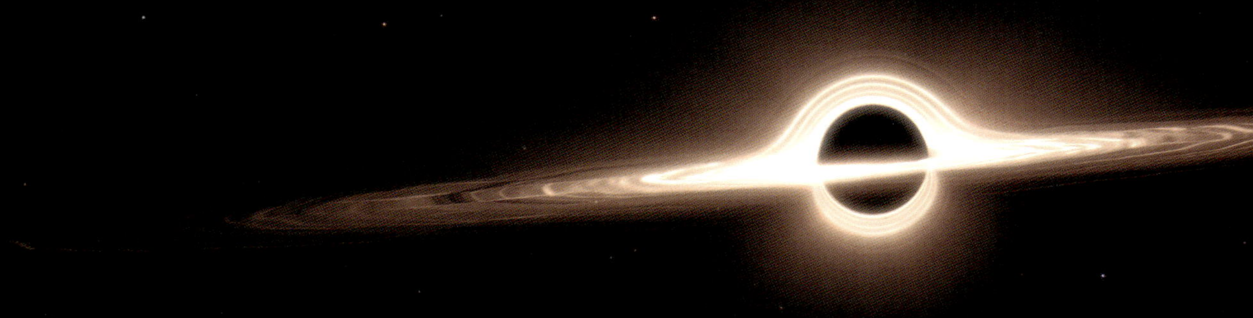

A black hole is a region of space where the gravitational force is so strong that nothing can escape from it. Thinking of wildly waving your hands to signal help? Well too bad. Black holes are invisible.

Why do lions attack humans?

Lions don't like us.

But not so much that they want to kill us. They tend to attack humans only if they are threatened or injured. The real question should be "Why do humans attack lions?"

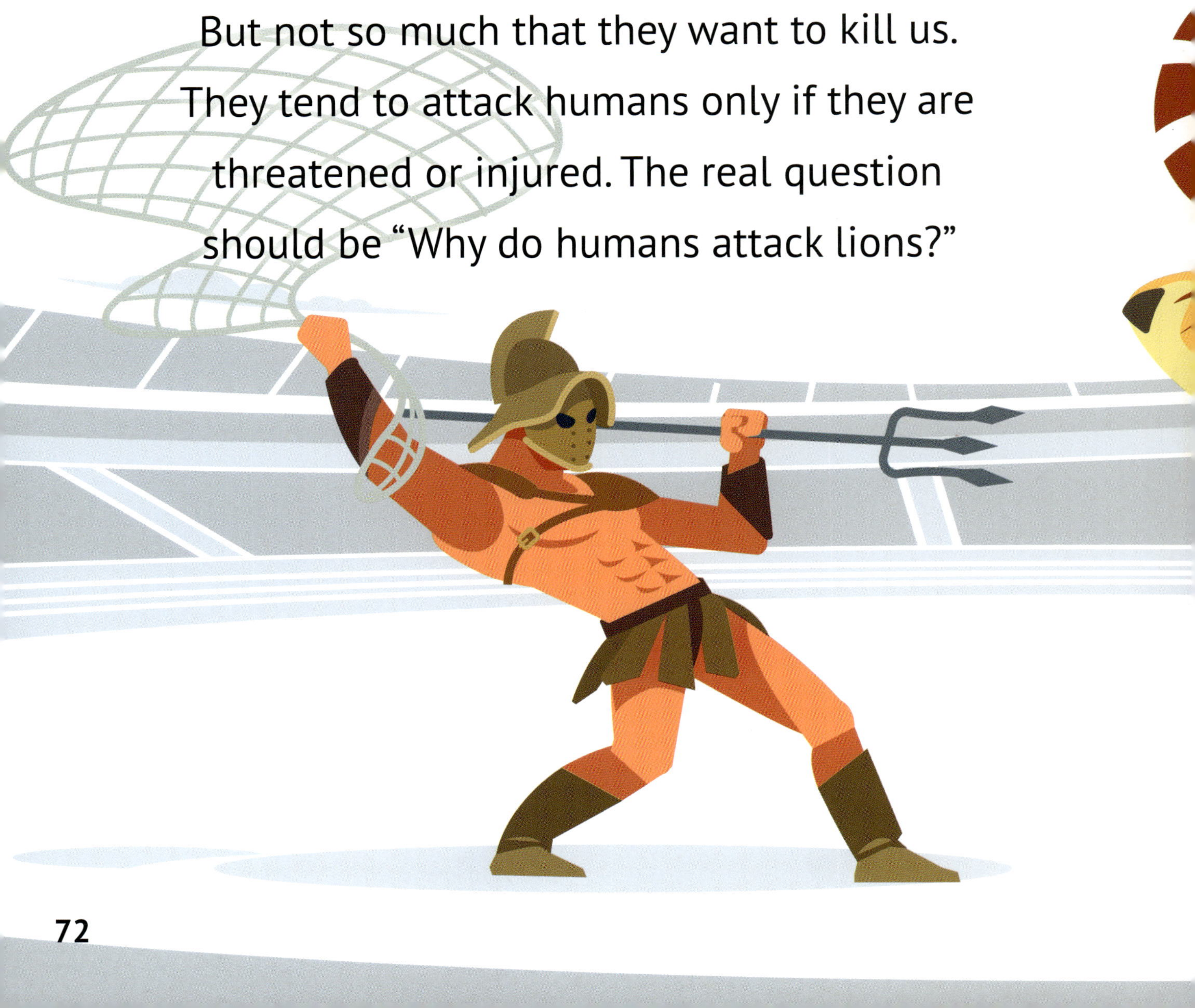

People kill lions much more frequently than lions kill humans. Lions think that it would be **roar-**some if humans stayed away from them.

What are tears made of?

Mostly water and salt.

Tears also contain proteins that fight bacteria and other germs. Sometimes tears are caused by sad emotions. But don't worry, tears aren't always associated with **tear**able feelings. You can also cry from laughter.

Do we eat our teeth?

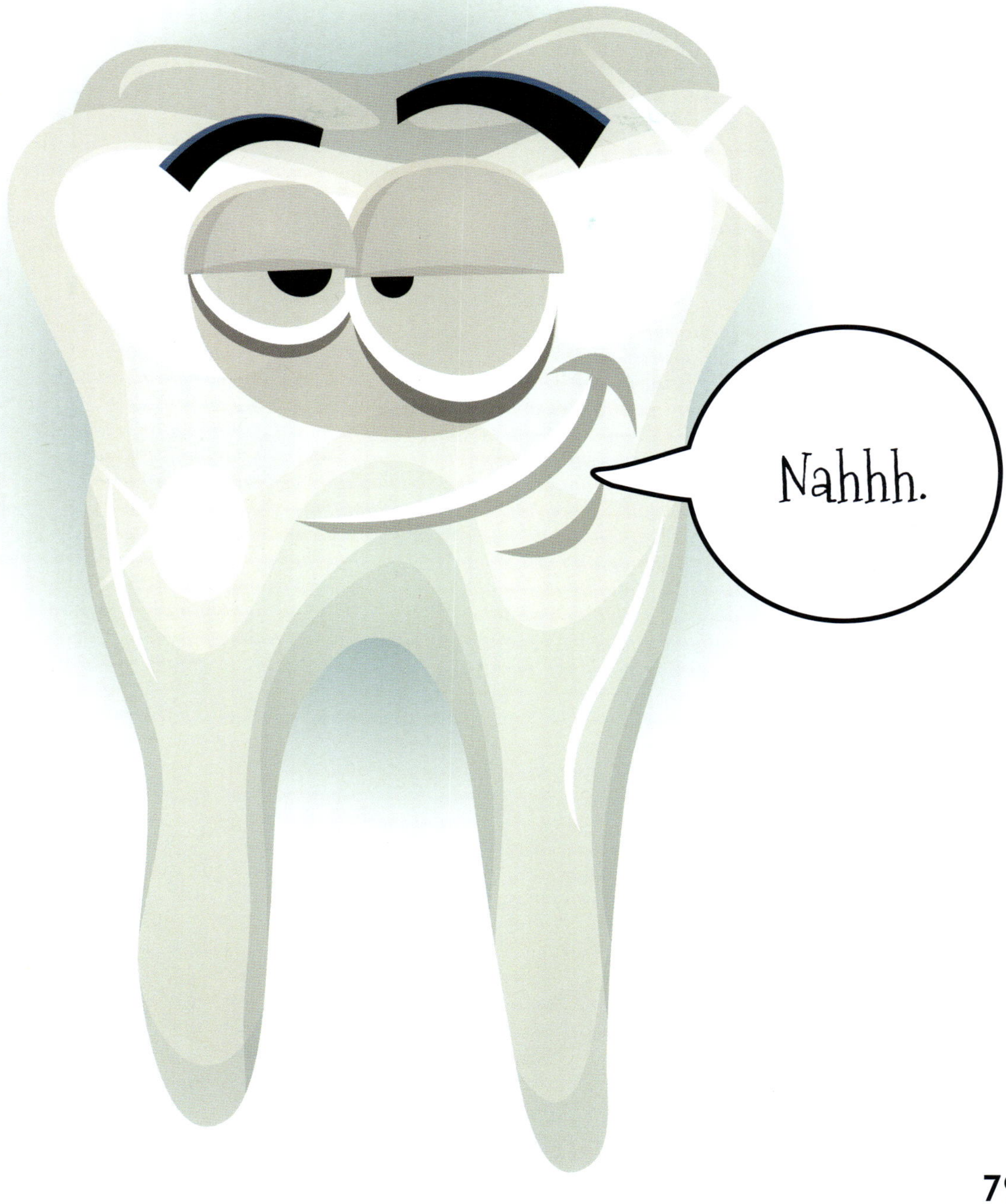
Nahhh.

It happens.

That doesn't mean we suggest you reach into your mouth when you're craving something crunchy. We mean that some people might on rare occasions swallow a bit of tooth. Young kids, for example, might accidentally swallow a baby tooth. No fear, a set of teeth won't grow in your stomach. The small object will pass through your digestive system.

Why do people tell ghost stories?

You've got to do something while you roast marshmallows around the campfire.

If you don't, you'll focus on the ghost right behind you! Ahhhh! Ghost stories play on fears of death, discomfort, or creepy places. Storytellers might be doing you a favor: the reminder of death might make your life—and your s'more—taste sweeter.

Why are there bears?

Because they're good at what they do.

Like all living things, bears exist because they're good at surviving in a specific role. Bears also help to maintain their ecosystem. By eating fruits and nuts, for example, bears help to spread plant seeds. Because of their incredible size and speed, bears could easily plow through a defensive line. The same can't always be said of the Chicago Bears of professional football.

Should I be afraid?

You just read a book about fears and dangers. Now you might want to hide inside and shelter from the scary world. The phrase "Be afraid, be very afraid" might be occupying your thoughts. But don't be afraid! As you just read, many fears are based on misunderstanding. The world is also filled with happy and joyous things, and they deserve your attention, too!

ENGAGE YOUR READER

GUIDED READING PROMPTS

Before Reading

- Allow readers to scan the text and discuss what they notice so far. Highlight the Question-and-Answer structure of this text and discuss a plan for reading.
- Explain the literacy skill: *Asking and answering questions helps us learn new information about the world around us! We can think more critically and deeply when we use higher levels of questions.*

During Reading

- Read each question and provide time to discuss readers' answers before turning the page to learn the facts. Did any of the facts surprise your readers?
- Practice the skills of retelling and summarizing by prompting your readers to rephrase the answer found in the text in their own words.
- Encourage readers to ask their own questions: *Now that you know this, what other related questions do you have?*

After Reading

- Prompt your readers to connect, extend, and challenge their thinking about the text:
  - *How are these ideas connected to what you already knew?*
  - *What new ideas did you get that extended or pushed your thinking in new directions?*
  - *What ideas are still challenging you? What questions, wonders, or puzzles do you still have?*

LOOK BACK!

What other examples of Level 1, 2, and 3 questions can you find in this text?

COMMON CORE CONNECTIONS

These questions and tasks align with the following Common Core College and Career Readiness Anchor Standards for Reading:

- CCSS.ELA-Literacy.CCRA.R.1
- CCSS.ELA-Literacy.CCRA.R.4
- CCSS.ELA-Literacy.CCRA.R.5
- CCSS.ELA-Literacy.CCRA.R.10

LITERACY SKILL

Asking and answering high level questions helps us think critically!

Check out Costa's Levels of Questioning:

- Level 1 – basic questions that help you gather information
  - Includes defining, describing, and identifying
- Level 2 – intermediate questions that help you process information
  - Includes explaining, inferring, and classifying
- Level 3 – more advanced questions that help you apply information
  - Includes evaluating, generalizing, and speculating

Examples from the text:

- Level 1 – p. 30-33 – Does your heart stop when you sneeze?
- Level 2 – p. 58-61 – What makes spiders dangerous?
- Level 3 – p. 34-37 – What would happen if an asteroid hit Earth?

EXTEND THROUGH WRITING

Ask your readers what they wonder about fear and danger.

- Have readers determine whether their questions involve gathering, processing, or applying information.
- Direct readers to create at least two Level 1, 2, and 3 questions about fear and danger.
- Challenge readers to research, determine the answers, and record them alongside the questions.

MORE WAYS TO ENGAGE!

- Create a question web by drawing a spider web on a piece of paper or by creating one out of yarn or rope. Encourage readers to practice asking questions while reading. When they come to a question, they can write it on a sticky note and add it to the web! Revisit these questions, determine their Costa's Level of Questioning, and work to find the answers together.
- Discuss what information in the book really took your readers by surprise and why they were not expecting that answer.

World Book, Inc.
180 North LaSalle Street
Suite 900
Chicago, Illinois 60601
USA

Copyright © 2023 (print and e-book) World Book, Inc. All rights reserved.

This volume may not be reproduced in whole or in part in any form without prior written permission from the publisher.

WORLD BOOK and the GLOBE DEVICE are registered trademarks or trademarks of World Book, Inc.

For information about other "Answer Me This, World Book" titles, as well as other World Book print and digital publications, please go to www.worldbook.com.

For information about other World Book publications, call 1-800-WORLDBK (967-5325).

For information about sales to schools and libraries, call 1-800-975-3250 (United States) or 1-800-837-5365 (Canada).

Library of Congress Cataloging-in-Publication Data for this volume has been applied for.

Answer Me This, World Book
ISBN: 978-0-7166-4675-4 (set, hc.)

If you sneeze with your eyes open, will they pop out?
World Book answers your questions about fear and danger
ISBN: 978-0-7166-4677-8 (hc.)

Also available as:
ISBN: 978-0-7166-4687-7 (e-book)

Printed in India by Thomson Press (India) Limited,
Uttar Pradesh, India
1st printing June 2022

Acknowledgments

Cover: © Master1305/Shutterstock; © Durantelallera/Shutterstock
2-94 © Shutterstock

Staff

Editorial

Writer
Madeline King

Senior Manager, New Content
Jeff De La Rosa

Manager, New Product
Nick Kilzer

Senior Content Creator
William D. Adams

Curriculum Designer
Caroline Davidson

Proofreader
Nathaniel Lindstrom

Graphics and Design

Senior Visual Communications Designer
Melanie Bender

Coordinator, Design Development and Production
Brenda Tropinski

Senior Media Editor
Rosalia Bledsoe